WOMEN OF SPORTS

THE BEST OF THE BEST *in* Gymnastics

BY
RACHEL RUTLEDGE

M
THE MILLBROOK PRESS
BROOKFIELD, CONNECTICUT

Produced by
CRONOPIO PUBLISHING
John Sammis, President
and
TEAM STEWART, INC.

Series Design and Electronic Page Makeup by
JAFFE ENTERPRISES
Ron Jaffe

Researched and Edited by
Mark Stewart, Michael Kennedy and Mariah Morgan

All photos courtesy
AP/WIDE WORLD PHOTOS, INC.
except the following:
EILEEN LANGSLEY/SUPERSPORT — Pages 22, 32, 44
DAVE BLACK — Pages 25, 46

Printed in the United States of America

Published by
The Millbrook Press, Inc.
2 Old New Milford Road
Brookfield, Connecticut 06804

Library of Congress Cataloging-in-Publication Data

Rutledge, Rachel.
  Women of Sports. The best of the best in gymnastics / by Rachel Rutledge.
     p.   cm.
  Includes index.
  Summary: Discusses the past and future of women's gymnastics and presents biographies of
eight of the sport's most famous players: Simona Amanar, Vanessa Atler, Dominique Dawes,
Ling Jie, Svetlana Khorkina, Kris Maloney, Shannon Miller, and Dominique Moceanu.
  ISBN 0-7613-1321-4 (lib. bdg.).—ISBN 0-7613-0784-2 (pbk.)
  1. Gymnasts—Biography—Juvenile literature. 2. Women gymnasts—Biography—Juvenile
literature. 3. Gymnastics for women—Juvenile literature. [1. Gymnasts. 2. Women—
Biography. 3. Gymnastics for women] I. Title.   II. Title: Best of the best in gymnastics.
GV460.R88 1999
796.44'082'092—dc21
[B]   98-51657
                                                                                        CIP
                                                                                        AC

pbk: 10 9 8 7 6 5 4 3 2 1
lib: 10 9 8 7 6 5 4 3 2 1

CONTENTS

In the Beginning

F ans of women's gymnastics insist that for sheer excitement, drama, and beauty, no other sport comes close. Anyone who has spent time around world-class gymnasts, or just watched them for a while on television, would find it hard to argue the point. Just about every sport demands power, grace, and precision from the human body, but in gymnastics these are the qualities that are specifically *used* to distinguish one athlete from another.

Unlike other sports where contestants are judged in these areas, there is no "outside force" exerting itself on gymnasts. Figure skating, for example, is what it is because of ice—or at least the lack of friction it creates. Diving is a sport that is essentially a battle against gravity. In gymnastics, most of the energy is generated by the bodies of the athletes. Friction and gravity play only minor roles.

When did gymnastics actually begin? Nobody knows for sure. We do know that the first Olympics were held in Greece in 776 B.C., but that it would be many years before an actual gymnastics competition was included. It was less a competitive sport at this time than it was a regimen of training. One of the favorite spectator sports of the ancients, however, was bull-jumping, which required an athlete to run toward a bull, grab its horns, and then flip high in the air and land standing on the bull's back.

This activity predates the Olympics, so if you consider it a risky version of the vault, you could say that gymnastics are more than 3,000 years old. The first gymnastics "meets" probably began about 2,500 years ago.

The term "gymnastics" is derived from the Greek word *gymnos*, which means "naked." That is because athletes competed in the nude back then.

How did women fit into this picture? They didn't. In fact, if a woman was caught trying to sneak into the Olympics, the punishment was spelled out quite succinctly: She was to be hurled off a cliff.

Gymnastics went into decline after the Romans conquered Greece. The sport was abolished altogether by Emperor Theodosius in 393 A.D. He believed that the empire's best athletes should be in the army, and no doubt felt threatened by a nation of fitness freaks just across the Aegean Sea. It would be 14 centuries before the sport reappeared.

Fast-forward to the 18th century. A couple of European professors managed to convince people that physical exercise—which had long been regarded as unhealthy and dangerous—was actually good for them. The only problem was that these two men, Frederick Jahn and Peter Ling, could not seem to agree on anything. Jahn thought strength training was the way to go, while Ling believed that exercises should focus on technique and precision. The one thing on which they did seem to agree was that none of this was suitable for women. Eventually, their competing theories were combined, marking the birth of modern gymnastics.

In 1896, when the Olympic Games were revived, gymnastics was one of the nine sports. Predictably, women were not included. That did not change until 1928, when the first Olympic women's team competition was held. No individual medals were awarded, but at least it was a start.

The watershed year for women's gymnastics did not come until 1952. That was the first year women competed in individual events in the Olympics, and the first year the Soviet Union sent teams to the Summer Games. Eastern European athletes dominated the competition for the

Russian star Larissa Latynina brought ballet-like moves to the sport in the 1950s and '60s. She won nine Olympic gold medals during her career.

next quarter-century, thanks to the government-sponsored sports training centers that sprang up behind the "Iron Curtain" after World War II.

The most successful gymnast of the 1950s was Hungary's Agnes Keleti, who captured 10 Olympic medals before defecting to the West in 1956. The most influential gymnast was Larissa Latynina of the Soviet Union. A classically trained ballerina, she brought grace and beauty to a sport that placed a high value on physical strength and still looked a lot like men's gymnastics at times. Latynina won five medals at the 1956 Olympics, and then won a medal in every event in 1960 and again in 1964. Latynina believed that risky maneuvers and routines emphasizing raw athleticism were antithetical to gymnastics. With so many medals to her credit, who would dare to argue? So for more than 15 years, the stars of women's gymnastics were not heart-stopping young risk-takers, but conservative, technically sound veterans in their 20s and early 30s. Basically, the sport was dull as dishwater.

That changed dramatically in 1972, at the Summer Games in Munich. The Soviet team, led by Lyudmila Tourischeva, rolled into the Olympics favored to take the lion's share of the medals. But as the competition unfolded, it was a Soviet alternate named Olga Korbut who stole the show. When the team arrived, the 85-pound Korbut was not even scheduled to compete. But an injury to a teammate gave her a chance.

Korbut did not look like the world's idea of a gymnast. She didn't even look like a *grownup*. She lacked the powerful, flowing lines of her more mature teammates, and wore pigtails knotted with strands of colored yarn. She even had the temerity to smile at the audience! The 17-year-old sprite did things on the balance beam no one had ever seen before, and she delighted the crowd with her imaginative and joyful floor exercise. She flew through the air on the vault and seemed unfettered by gravity on the uneven bars. Korbut looked like she would win the all-arounds until she botched several moves on the uneven bars. The television camera followed her to the sideline, where she sobbed uncontrollably. At that moment the world fell in love with her—her youth, her innocence, and her honesty—and gymnastics changed forever.

In 1972, Olga Korbut captured the world's attention by doing something no one else in the sport dared to try: smiling.

The result of Korbut's magnificent performance was a period of turmoil in Soviet gymnastics, as Tourischeva and rising star Nelli Kim bristled at

Nadia Comaneci concludes her perfect 10 performance on the uneven bars during the 1976 Olympics.

the special privileges Korbut demanded and got. By the time the 1976 Olympics started, the team was thoroughly demoralized. Into this void stepped 14-year-old Nadia Comaneci, who earned seven perfect 10s and won three gold medals. Though not as captivating as Korbut, the young Romanian was supremely athletic and absolutely fearless, completing daring moves that most of her competitors would not even consider trying.

In the United States, gymnastics had been a dead issue for most of the 1950s and '60s. Americans had no interest in a sport so clearly dominated by Communist countries, especially during the chilliest days of the Cold War. But the performances of Korbut and Comaneci, as well as U.S. star

Cathy Rigby, turned an entire generation of young American girls on to competitive gymnastics. As the sport grew quickly at the grass-roots level in the United States, gym ownership and elite-level coaching became lucrative businesses. This lured some of the best coaches in the world to America, where they began working with some exceptional young athletes.

This "revolution" first bore fruit in 1984. Mary Lou Retton, the diminutive daughter of a former college basketball star, and Bela Karolyi, who had coached Nadia Comaneci, joined forces and struck gold at the Los Angeles Olympics. Other U.S. medal winners in '84 included Kathy Johnson and Julianne Mc-Namara, while the U.S. team itself took the silver behind the Romanians. The Soviet Union had boycotted the games, so the medals were somewhat tainted, but the team's success only increased interest in the sport in the United States.

After a poor showing at the 1988 Olympics, Team USA rebounded with an overall bronze medal in 1992. More important, the

Mary Lou Retton can barely contain her emotions after a gold-medal performance at the 1984 Olympics.

young gymnasts on that team—Dominique Dawes, Shannon Miller, Kerri Strug, and Kim Zmeskal—would form the nucleus of the 1996 Olympic team. Rounding out the '96 squad were Dominique Moceanu, Jaycie Phillips, and Amy Chow.

All of these names are familiar to fans now, of course, but prior to the games in Atlanta people in gymnastics saw one thing when they looked at the '96 Olympians: a team without a superstar. It was also hard to imagine seven young women more different from the ones who comprised Team USA.

Ironically, these "shortcomings" turned out to be their greatest strengths. Because no one personality dominated the team, each girl felt free to be herself and approach her task in her own way. And because no one could relax and rely on a superior teammate, there was never any thought about letting up. Thus every time an American gymnast performed a routine, she knew she had to give the performance of her life. With few exceptions, that is what happened. The Russian and Romanian teams, favorites to fight it out for the gold and silver, watched in dismay as their fist-pumping, high-fiving foes absorbed the energy of the Georgia Dome crowd and used it to power their performances.

By the final rotation, Team USA had built a seemingly insurmountable lead. But disaster struck in the vault, as Dominique Moceanu missed badly on both of her attempts. Then Kerri Strug missed her first attempt, badly hurting her ankle in the process. Knowing that she would face excruciating pain—and perhaps a career-ending injury—Strug decided to do her last vault anyway. She nailed it to secure gold for the U.S. team, and left her indelible mark on the 1996 Summer Games as she was carried off the mat by her coach, Bela Karolyi.

How magnificent were the "Magnificent Seven?" In terms of its achievement, the U.S. team lived up to its nickname: What those young women pulled off was indeed magnificent. Fans are quick to forget that only three of them (Miller, Dawes, and Chow) were good enough to win

The U.S. women's gymnastics team waves to the crowd after being awarded their gold medals in the team competition at the 1996 Olympic Games in Atlanta. From left are Amanda Borden, Dominique Dawes, Amy Chow, Jaycie Phelps, Dominique Moceanu, Kerri Strug, and Shannon Miller.

individual medals, while a total of 12 medals went to members of rival teams. Athlete-for-athlete, there is no way Team USA should have won.

Three of the women on the 1996 women's national team are featured in this book, along with two of America's most promising young gymnasts. You will also find profiles of three other young stars from the powerhouse programs in Russia, China, and Romania. As a group, these eight athletes provide an interesting perspective on the past, present, and future of women's gymnastics.

Legendary coach Bela Karolyi carries an injured Kerri Strug at the Olympic medal ceremony. Dominique Moceanu, another Karolyi pupil, is at left.

4 Events—18 Medals

Gymnastics meets come in all shapes and sizes, but they all are based on four specific events: the vault, uneven parallel bars, balance beam, and floor exercise. In a typical international meet, team competition is held in these four areas on the first day, with three medals up for grabs: gold, silver, and bronze. On the second day, the highest-scoring women in each event (as established during the team competition) come back to compete for a total of 12 individual medals. And on the final day, the very best competitors return to vie for the title of best all-around gymnast. Add up all the medals and you have a grand total of 18. Of course, some meets are team-only affairs, while others feature purely individual competition. Many one-day meets roll everything into one, determining individual-event and all-around winners from scores achieved during the team competition. Regardless of how a meet is conducted, these are the important things to know about the various events.

VAULT

Judges look at three elements—the support (or pushing-off) phase, the flight phase, and the landing. The more twists and tumbles, and the higher the jump, the greater the score. A penalty is assessed for extra steps on the landing.

UNEVEN BARS

Judges score based on a long checklist of characteristics, including grip changes, releases and regrasps, flight elements, changes of direction, and circle swings through the handstand position. A routine must flow without pauses or extra swings, and must have at least two release elements.

BALANCE BEAM

Judges look for two types of movements—an acrobatic series (such as a cartwheel into a back handspring) and a gymnastic series (such as a turn followed by a split jump). There are a number of required moves, and judges also look for dance influences. A beam routine must last between 70 and 90 seconds and cover the entire length of the 4-inch-wide apparatus.

FLOOR EXERCISE

Judges look for a blend of acrobatic and gymnastic elements, as well as use of floor. Set to music, this event allows an athlete to express her timing and grace in a highly personal and entertaining way.

ALL-AROUNDS

A compilation of scores from the four events described above. The key here, as in any multi-event sports competition, is consistency.

TEAM COMPETITION

A competition consisting of four "rotations"—vault, bars, beam, and floor exercise. A predetermined number of team members compete in each event, and their scores are averaged and compiled after each rotation. The team with the highest combined score wins.

Simona
Amanar

Gymnastics is not a sport known for its "team players." That is why Kerri Strug made such a sensation when she went for her final, unforgettable vault at the 1996 Olympics. In the Georgia Dome that evening, watching along with the rest of the world, was Romania's Simona Amanar, the finest vaulter on the planet. She knew why Strug did what she did. That kind of team spirit has been within Simona as long as anyone can remember.

Simona rose from humble beginnings. She was born in 1979, in the town of Constanta, on the coast of the Black Sea. Her father, Vasile, labored long hours for little money in a local factory. Her mother, Sofia, cared for Simona and her brother, Andrei. There was not always enough to eat, and the simple things we sometimes take for granted—such as new shoes and supplies for school—were not always available. Born into a system that offered little hope of improvement for a family like the Amanars, Simona's future looked pretty bleak.

That is, until she went on a 1985 outing. "When I was about five or six, I went to see a gymnastics competition in my hometown of Constanta," Simona remembers. "It looked like so much fun I went to the gym. I liked it straight away, and decided to carry on."

One of the advantages of living in Romania was that sports programs were free. The government viewed success in international sports as a

Simona pushes off on a vault at the 1998 Goodwill Games, where she earned a bronze medal in the event.

Four Romanian medalists wave to the crowd at the 1996 Olympics; left to right, Simona, Lavinia Milosovici, Lilla Podkopayeva, and Gina Gogean.

source of great national pride, and thus encouraged as many children as possible to get involved at an early age. From the thousands of promising athletes that developed, a few dozen of the very best were selected and moved to national training centers, where they were groomed for the national team. Simona did not understand or care about the politics. She was just happy to have something that she enjoyed doing—and glad that it was not costing her parents any money.

Simona's instincts for gymnastics and her love of competition soon caught the eye of coach Nicolae Forminte. "When she was ten years old," he says, "I knew she would be good."

He was correct. Within two years, Simona was moved to the national training center in the city of Deva. She was not happy about leaving her family and her home, but the prospect of getting better and competing for her country was just too tempting. She decided that a little homesickness was worth it. Simona credits her rapid development to the emotional support and training she received from the people in Deva, especially Octavian Belu, the national team coach. "From the beginning, the coaches said that I was a strong and powerful girl, so they encouraged me to continue," she says. Within two years, Simona had made the national team.

The youngest member of a powerful Romanian squad, 14-year-old Simona helped her country win three major competitions, including the European Championships. Most of the accolades went to teammates Lavinia Miloso-vici, Gina Gogean, and Alexandra Marinescu. They were famous international stars, and they loved the spotlight. Simona was just happy to have contributed, although gymnastics insiders were already whispering about the 4'-9" sprite who sat quietly at the end of the Romanian bench.

In 1995, the secret got out. Simona came into her own, especially in the vault. Her powerful take-offs and heart-stopping midair acrobatics brought crowds to their feet everywhere the team competed. Her big breakthrough enabled the Romanian team to dominate, winning four international events. Simona, who won the vault at the World Championships for her first major individual victory, was poised on the threshold of greatness. Actually, the growing attention Simona received made her uncomfortable. To her, gymnastics was a *team* sport. You did your best as an individual competitor so your *team* could get

Getting Personal

As a child, Simona was inspired by fellow Romanian Nadia Comaneci. She sometimes watches videos of Comaneci at the 1976 Olympics...Simona is the ideal size for a vaulter. She stands a shade under 4'-10" and weighs around 85 pounds...She is known for her supreme sportsmanship. After a disappointing second-place finish in the all-arounds at the 1997 World Championships, she congratulated winner Svetlana Khorkina and thanked her coaches for helping her do so well...Traveling to meets around the world enables her to hit music stores and stock up on CDs of her favorite artists, Mariah Carey and Tina Turner...Her favorite movie star is Jean-Claude Van Damme. Her favorite athlete is French figure skater Surya Bonaly, who also is known for her midair acrobatics...Simona joined the World Gymnastics Tour at the end of 1998, performing with Kerri Strug and other top gymnasts throughout the United States. Before the fall of Communism in her country, Simona would have been forbidden to join this tour...Thanks to Simona's success, her family is no longer impoverished. In fact, the Amanars now live in a lovely apartment overlooking the Black Sea, and drive a luxury car.

Career *Highlights*

Year	Achievement
1994	Gold Medalist, European Championships, Team Competition
1995	Gold Medalist, World Championships, Vault & Team Competition
1996	Gold Medalist, European Championships, Vault, Uneven Bars, & Team Competition
1996	Olympic Gold Medalist, Vault
1996	Olympic Silver Medalist, Floor Exercise
1996	Olympic Bronze Medalist, All-Arounds
1996	Olympic Bronze Medalist, Team Competition
1997	Gold Medalist, World Championships, Vault, & Team Competition
1998	Gold Medalist, European Championships, Vault, Balance Beam, & Floor Exercise
1998	Gold Medalist, World Cup, Vault
1998	Silver Medalist, Goodwill Games, Floor Exercise
1998	Gold Medalist, European Championships, Team Competition

the most points. If you happened to do better than any of the other women, that was merely a bonus.

The "bonuses" began piling up for Simona in 1996. At the European Championships, she finished first in the vault and uneven bars, and performed brilliantly in leading Romania to a team gold medal. At the Olympics, Simona's star continued to shine. She executed an eye-popping vault during the team competition to put Romania within a single point of first place. In the end, though, the surprising Americans and always-tough Russians managed to hang on to the top two spots, so Romania had to settle for a bronze medal. Simona, however, was just getting started. She won gold in the vault, silver in the floor exercise, and bronze in the all-arounds.

Several months later, Romania gained some measure of revenge by winning at the 1997 World Championships by the largest margin ever. Again, Simona turned in a thrilling performance in the vault. "I was last up," she remembers, "and I knew I had to do the best two vaults of my life." Ever the clutch performer, Simona nailed both to win the world title.

With Milosovici and Gogean retired, the 1998 season was a pivotal one for Simona. Like it or not, she was now the focal point of the Romanian national team. She turned in another great year, leading many to wonder how long she can maintain her incredible run and how good she will ultimately become. Not surprisingly, Simona responds to queries about her future with thoughts about the team. She will be as good as she can be, she says, and compete as long as she can compete. The important thing is that she sees good prospects coming up behind her.

Why, you might wonder, would Simona care about girls who won't see the light of competition until long after she retires?

That's easy.

"I want to be a coach!" she smiles.

Simona's performance on the beam helped her win a bronze medal in the all-arounds at the 1996 Olympics.

"They say young people can't handle the pressure, but I proved I can handle it."

Vanessa Atler

Vanessa Atler was born on February 17, 1982. That is probably the best-known birthday in American gymnastics, for it
has put the young woman everyone calls "Nessa" at the heart
of a raging controversy. Prior to the 1996 season, a minimum age was set
for participants in international events, including the Olympics. That age
was 15, which meant Vanessa was seven weeks too young to go to Atlanta.
A year later, prior to the 1997 season, the cut-off was raised to *16*, meaning she got nailed again. "The rule is kind of stupid," says Vanessa, who
is finally old enough to compete on the senior level.

Although the age requirement was created to help young gymnasts, it
hurt Vanessa. She was a world-class competitor in every imaginable way
by the age of 14, and one of the best in the world at age 15. Today, she is
the leading light in American gymnastics. Elegant, mature, and utterly
fearless, Vanessa has the quickness of a cat and the heart of a lioness.

Vanessa has dreamed of performing in front of a cheering crowd for as
long as she can remember. Originally, though, her goal was to become a
cheerleader. Her parents decided to enroll her in a tumbling class, and
soon she was the best kid in the gym. In her first competitive event, at
age five, Vanessa not only won her age group, she scored higher than anyone else at the meet. From tumbling, she moved into gymnastics, joining
the Charter Oak Gym in Covina, California.

Vanessa liked Charter Oak because it was less intense than other gymnastics centers. Parents were allowed to observe training sessions, and the

*Vanessa waves to the crowd after receiving the
gold medal in the vault at the 1998 Goodwill Games.*

Vanessa's poise in the floor exercise makes it hard to believe she was ever considered too young to compete.

girls were not weighed—practices that ran contrary to standard policy in most gyms. Vanessa was coached by the husband-wife team of Steve and Beth Rybacki. Beth had been a member of the 1980 U.S. Olympic team when she was 14 (there were no age restrictions back then) and knew a thing or two about the unfairness of rules. She had a chance to win a medal that year, but the U.S. team boycotted the Olympics and she never got the opportunity.

Vanessa took to gymnastics in a big way—especially the tougher events, such as the balance beam. She kind of liked the challenge of knowing that one minuscule error could send her crashing to the mat. In 1991, another talented newcomer, Jamie Dantzscher, joined the gym, and she and Vanessa became fast friends. "We are a team," says Vanessa. "We're like sisters."

When it became clear that 11-year-old Vanessa had Olympic potential, her parents took her out of school and set her up in an independent study program. The idea was to give her the best possible training schedule (five to six hours a day) while working academics around her gymnastics. A superb student, Vanessa did so well that she had to be slowed down—she was on track to graduate high school during her sophomore year!

By 1994, Vanessa was holding her own in top junior competition. In 1995, she got her first taste of success on the international level, when she finished second in the vault and third in the floor exercise at the Catania Cup in Italy. Later that season, Vanessa traveled to Japan for the International Junior Gymnastics Competition and finished first in the floor exercise. She was on her way.

The 1996 season was one of both satisfaction and frustration for Vanessa. She won the all-arounds at the U.S. Junior Championships, attacking each event and dazzling the crowd. "I was proud of my bar routine because I was most aggressive on this event," she remembers. "I was *most* proud of my beam routine, because it's a hard event to do, and it was last, and I stayed under control."

Because of the new minimum age rules, Vanessa knew she could not compete in the Olympics. At the beginning of the year, this was not an issue because she assumed she was not good enough to make the U.S. team. But as the season unfolded, it became clear that she was as good as—if not *better* than—many of the athletes competing for spots on the Olympic squad. At the American Classic in Tulsa, Oklahoma, Vanessa

Getting Personal

Sports run in Vanessa's family. Her parents are big tennis players, her brother, Teddy, loves baseball, and her second cousin, Joe Kapp, quarterbacked the Minnesota Vikings to the Super Bowl one year...Vanessa is one-quarter Mexican...She was the first woman to go from U.S. junior champion to U.S. senior champion in one year since Dominique Moceanu...Vanessa took acting lessons and auditioned for a role in the film version of "Little Girls in Pretty Boxes." Although she did not get a speaking part, she worked as a stunt double...Vanessa's two gold medals at the 1998 Goodwill Games were twice as many as the combined total won by the U.S. men's and women's teams in the previous three competitions...She trains six days a week— about 35 hours—a little more before a big meet. Her daily regimen includes 300 stomach crunches...There are, Vanessa admits, some downsides to being the rising star of American gymnastics. She does not go to a lot of parties, she does not have classmates like most kids, and her schedule keeps her from socializing as much as she would like...She closed out a great '98 season with four gold medals at the Australia Cup...Being the leader of America's next wave of world-class gymnasts is appealing to Vanessa, especially after missing out on the chance to be one of the "Magnificent Seven" in 1996. "Now it's our chance to be on TV and be all famous and stuff."

Career *Highlights*

Year	Achievement
1995	Gold Medalist, US Olympic Festival, Balance Beam
1995	Silver Medalist, US Junior Championships, All-Arounds & Uneven Bar
1996	Gold Medalist, US Junior Championships, All-Arounds
1997	Gold Medalist, American Cup, Vault & Balance Beam
1997	Gold Medalist, US Championships, All-Arounds & Vault
1998	Gold Medalist, International Team Championships
1998	Gold Medalist, Goodwill Games, Vault
1998	Gold Medalist, American Cup, Vault

won the all-arounds and posted scores high enough to qualify her for the Olympic trials—and earn her a spot on the U.S. World Championship team. "When I realized I could have made the world team," she says, "I got mad at the people who made this rule."

In 1997, Vanessa experienced the same kind of success and frustration. As the U.S. Championships began, the question everyone was asking was "Who will step up to become the next major force in American gymnastics?" Vanessa answered that question by winning the vault and finishing in a first-place tie with Kristy Powell in the all-arounds. She was a mile ahead of Powell going into the final event, the uneven bars, but lost her concentration and received a low score.

Vanessa had entered the nationals mainly for the experience. She knew she was still too young to go to the World Championships, but she wanted to see what she could do—and learn—competing against older athletes. Vanessa also entered the 1997 American Cup, hoping to show her stuff in the sport's first major meet since the '96 Olympics. All she did was win the vault and beam events, and lose the all-around title by just seven one-thousandths of a point.

Suddenly, the world was looking at Vanessa differently. Requests for interviews poured in and hits on her Web site went through the roof. Everyone wanted to know everything about her. At meets, she could feel a difference, too. Instead of people wishing her luck, they would ask her if she thought she was going to win. "Before winning the nationals it was a lot different," she says. "Only a few people interviewed me, a few phone calls, and an average amount of fan mail. Every competition now, I realize that second place doesn't make the public happy anymore."

Vanessa's 1998 year was what everyone was hoping for, and then some. In the season's biggest event, the Goodwill Games, she displayed great maturity and poise as she won the floor exercise, and surprised Simona Amanar by taking gold in the vault. The biggest highlight of 1998 for Vanessa, however, was Team USA's victory over the Romanians at the International Team Championships. In a sport so focused on individual effort she is, first and foremost, a team player.

Vanessa's gold medals at the Goodwill Games underscored her growth as a person and performer, and sent a signal to the gymnastics world that she is capable of surpassing the expectations of even her most ardent supporters. All that remains now is to learn how to produce these wonderful performances meet after meet after meet. Vanessa knows that is the difference between a great athlete and a great *champion*. "I'm working on consistency," she says.

The focus now shifts to the 2000 Olympics. As she sees it, the key to doing well is to not get wrapped up in the aura of the event. "I want to have a great life, and my happiness isn't about whether or not I'm in the Olympics," Vanessa maintains. "But it would be a perfect ending."

Beyond the 2000 games, there is college and, of course, the rest of her life. What does Vanessa see when she peers into her crystal ball? She wants to stay in gymnastics, but *not* as a coach. What then?

"Maybe I'll be one of those people who makes the age limit decision," she cracks. "And this time I'll get it right!"

ZVanessa attempts a tricky release on the uneven bars.

Dominique Dawes

When historians look back on the remarkable rise of American gymnastics during the 1990s, they will no doubt credit Dominique Dawes with much of that success. Long before the "Magnificent Seven" captured the imagination of the sport at the 1996 Olympics, the young lady nicknamed "Awesome Dawesome" was the favorite gymnast of millions of young girls.

One of the most compelling aspects of Dominique's style is her ballet-like grace. That has much to do with the fact that she was taking dance lessons before she ever set foot in a gym. Dancing, however, did not adequately quench Dominique's thirst for action. To the considerable chagrin of her mom and dad, the six-year-old dynamo spent much of her time thundering up and down the stairs and leaping around the living room. Gymnastics classes seemed like the best way to wear out Dominique before she wore out the upholstery. "I had a lot of energy around the house," she grins. "My parents wanted me to use it someplace other than on the furniture."

The Daweses enrolled Dominique at the Marva Tots and Teens Gym, about 45 minutes away from their home in Silver Spring, Maryland. There she met Kelli Hill, who would become her coach. For several years, gymnastics was merely an activity for Dominique. The story has been told many times over of how she won every event in her first meet, but the truth of the matter is that she and her best friend were the only

Dominique was at the height of her powers when she captured the bronze medal in the floor exercise at the 1996 Olympics.

Media giant Ted Turner (left) and New York Governor George Pataki greet Dominique at an event publicizing the 1998 Goodwill Games.

competitors in the 10-year-old age group. "It was really funny," Dominique remembers. "We were falling all over the place."

Dominique became serious about gymnastics at age 11 or 12. She found that she got a tremendous charge out of executing difficult moves, and thrived on competition. As she grew stronger and more confident, she found she had tremendous spring in her legs—a huge plus in a sport where an athlete must accomplish much during the short time she is in the air. Dominique, who continued to take jazz and ballet classes, also possessed the kind of grace and style judges look for in big events. By the time she turned 14, it was clear she had a shot at making the 1992 Olympic team.

Coach Hill explained to Dominique that her training regimen would have to intensify. That meant early morning practices, which required her mom or dad to wake up at 4:30 A.M. and drive Dominique to the gym, and then later to school. This was not feasible, so the decision was made that she would live with the Hills. Dominique had to switch to a new school mid-semester, and she missed her old friends. She spent plenty of time on the weekends with her family, but the separation still was not easy. "We learned to deal with it," she says. "We were setting goals and everyone had to sacrifice a little bit. But the sacrifices were worth it."

Indeed they were. Dominique blossomed under this new arrangement, winning a gold medal at the 1991 nationals and making the '92 Olympic team. At 15, she was one of the youngest members of a very young squad.

Teammate Shannon Miller was also 15, while Kerri Strug was still 14. At the Summer Games in Barcelona, Team USA won a bronze medal. Dominique was an important contributor to this effort, but did not qualify for any of the individual events.

Now a "veteran" of top-flight international competition, Dominique had a much better idea of what it would take to become a top gymnast. She worked hard to improve in all areas, including her mental toughness. Before meets, she would write the words *Determination*, *Dedication,* and *Dynamics* on her bathroom mirror "to psyche me up and get me ready." She still subscribes to these ideas, which she calls her "3-D philosophy." At the 1993 World Championships, Dominique finished fourth in the all-arounds and won silver medals in the uneven bars and balance beam. At the U.S. Championships, she finished first in 'the beam and the vault.

Getting Personal

Dominique's mother is named Loretta, and her father's name is Don. They divorced when Dominique was 17...She has an older sister, Danielle, and a younger brother, Don, Jr....She came to Kelli Hill's gym by chance. The family first went to a local gym, and no other kids showed up. That evening, at a restaurant, they ran into a group from Marva Tots and Teens...In 1992, she became the first African-American woman to win an Olympic gymnastics medal...If there was an award for having your name in the most musical lyrics, Dominique would win it hands-down. In 1998 alone, she was in more than half a dozen rap and hip-hop cuts...Dominique was inducted into the Gymnastics Hall of Fame during the summer of 1998...She recently appeared in an ad for the American Heart Association with fellow legends Nadia Comaneci and Mary Lou Retton...In 1998, she was tabbed by SPORT magazine as the world's best-dressed female athlete.

In 1994, Dominique had one of the greatest seasons ever for an American gymnast, opening the year with gold medals in all five events at the American Cup and then repeating this feat at the U.S. Championships.

Then, as quickly as it had ascended, Dominique's star began to fall. She lost the 1995 season to a series of injuries, and some questioned whether she would even make the U.S. team for the 1996 Olympics. Dominique had to make a decision. Would she be happy being remembered as an athlete who had one unforgettable year? If not, was she willing

Career *Highlights*

Year	Achievement
1991	Gold Medalist, U.S. Championships, Floor Exercise
1992	Gold Medalist, U.S. Championships, Uneven Bars
1992	Olympic Bronze Medalist, Team Competition
1993	Gold Medalist, U.S. Championships, Vault & Balance Beam
1993	Silver Medalist, World Championships, Uneven Bars & Balance Beam
1994	Gold Medalist, U.S. Championships, Vault, Uneven Bars, Balance Beam, Floor Exercise, & All-Arounds
1994	Silver Medalist, World Championships, Team Competition
1995	Gold Medalist, U.S. Championships, Uneven Bars & Floor Exercise
1996	Gold Medalist, U.S. Championships, Vault, Uneven Bars, Balance Beam, & Floor Exercise
1996	Bronze Medalist, World Championships, Floor Exercise
1996	Olympic Gold Medalist, Team Competition
1996	Olympic Bronze Medalist, Floor Exercise
1998	Goodwill Games Participant

to put in the training required to return to the Olympics and do well there? Also, did it make sense to put off her college education to follow a dream?

Dominique decided to go for it. "I wanted people to remember me for my strong character," she says.

Month after month, Dominique hit the gym for three hours each morning and five more hours each evening. At the Olympic trials, the hard work showed, as she made the team easily. It was on to Atlanta, where Dominique had two goals: a team medal and an individual medal.

Team USA won the gold, and Dominique was a huge part of that effort. She killed on the uneven bars, the beam, and the floor exercise. In the vault, she nailed a tough jump and received a 9.762, which helped the Americans push ahead of the stunned Russians, into first place.

Later, in the individual events, Dominique went after some hardware of her own. She had qualified to compete in the vault, uneven bars, and all-arounds. When Kerri Strug had to bow out of the floor exercise, Dominique replaced her. With little time to prepare, Dominique used everything she had learned in 14 years of competitive gymnastics and put together a marvelous floor routine, surpassing all but two of the favorites to secure a bronze medal. "I was pretty pleased with that performance," she smiles.

After Atlanta, Dominique cut down on her schedule and attempted to blend back into a more normal life. This was easier said than done. When you are among the most recognized athletes in the country, opportunity always seems to knock. That winter, Dominique was bitten by the acting bug and landed a part in the Broadway production of *Grease!* In 1997, she embarked upon a 25-city gymnastics tour, and the following fall she began her freshman year at the University of Maryland.

In 1998, Dominique faced yet another decision: stay in competitive gymnastics another year or two, or pursue her education and her "next" career, whatever that may be. She rededicated herself to the sport and returned to peak form, tying for first-place in the vault at the American Cup and finishing third at the World Pro Championships. At the Goodwill Games, she entered the mixed pairs competition and finished eighth, then finished fifth in the uneven bars. Dominique seemed to be back on track when she unexpectedly pulled out of the U.S. Championships, and also canceled on the Rock & Roll Gymnastics Challenge. She said she wanted to take a couple of months off to think about her future in gymnastics.

Should she permanently retire from elite-level competition, Dominique may throw herself into acting, or find new interests in college and pursue those. She could also stay active in gymnastics, too—as a commentator, performer, or coach. One thing, how-ever, is certain. Whatever her decision, Dominique Dawes will no doubt find success, and inspire many more young girls before she is through.

Dominique's beam routine was one of four gold-medal performances she gave at the 1996 nationals.

Ling Jie

When you get right down to it, women's gymnastics is a "numbers" game. The more young girls a country can feed into the sport, the more talented athletes will emerge. And the more talented athletes a national program has to work with, the more world-class gymnasts it is likely to produce. This is a major reason why most people in gymnastics believe that the team to beat in the coming century will be China, a country with a population of more than a billion people. The first wave of this Chinese revolution is already sweeping over the sport, and its most promising young star is Ling Jie.

Jie was born in 1982, in the Heng-yang section of China's Hunan province. To control its population, China encouraged families to produce only one child, so she had no brothers and sisters. But that meant Jie was the main focus of her parents' love and attention. She first tried gymnastics at the age of three, when her father noticed an ad in a local newspaper. A nearby sports club was recruiting gymnasts, and he thought Jie would enjoy herself. She turned out to be a natural.

Jie possessed the qualities gymnastics coaches look for in young girls: she had grace, precision, concentration, and creativity. Around the age of eight, she began to truly distinguish herself. She responded beautifully to coaching, and seemed to have an instinct for pleasing judges, even in the heat of competition. She soon came to the attention of officials at China's

Jie has emerged as one of the leaders of China's national team.

*Jie's blend of power and creativity make her
tough to beat on the uneven bars.*

state-sponsored gymnastics training program, which approved govern-ment funding to further her development.

Eventually, Jie was deemed good enough to join China's other elite young gymnasts at the country's national training center, located in Beijing. In 1996, she began training and living with other promising gymnasts, all of whom hoped to make the national team. This situation may seem unusual to Americans, but it has long been the accepted system in Communist countries, such as China, the former Soviet Union, and many of the nations in Eastern Europe. By the time athletes are allowed to enter international competition, their technique is practically perfect. This accounts for the decades-long dominance of Soviets, Romanians, Hungarians, Czechs, and East Germans, and it is why China chose to base its sports system on this model. Where this system falls short, critics maintain, is that it stifles an athlete's creativity. With so much emphasis on technique, performances become almost robotic.

Getting Personal

Jie's parents are factory workers...She has had limited contact with her mom and dad since joining the national team in 1996. When she is not competing, she lives at the national training center in Beijing...Like most of the kids in the program, Jie has no brothers and sisters...She practices all day on Mondays, Wednesdays, and Fridays, as well as half-days on Tuesdays, Thursdays, and Saturdays. The rest of her time is spent on her studies...Sunday is Jie's day off. Ever dedicated, she usually puts in a couple of hours of running and aerobics...Her role models are Svetlana Khorkina of Russia and former champion Gina Gogean of Romania. "I admire their skills and consistency," she says.

It soon became clear that Jie was an exception to this rule. Whereas other girls could approach her exceptional technique, they seemed to lack the emotion Jie brought to her craft. She stands several inches under five feet, weighs about 70 pounds soaking wet, and has a high-energy, ant-on-a-hot-rock persona. Judges are not supposed to count "personality" when coming up with a final score, but even the most stone-hearted ones are invariably swayed by a "special" performance. This has helped Jie time and again.

Jie got her first taste of world-class competition at the age of 14. She traveled with the national team to a number of events, including the

Career *Highlights*

Year	Achievement
1997	Silver Medalist, International Team Championships, All-Arounds
1997	Gold Medalist, Chinese National Championships, Balance Beam & Uneven Bars
1998	Gold Medalist, Goodwill Games, Mixed Pairs
1998	Gold Medalist, World Cup, Team Competition
1998	Gold Medalist, China Cup, Balance Beam & Uneven Bars

1997 International Team Championships, in Knoxville, Tennessee. There, she opened a lot of eyes in the gymnastics world, scoring phenomenally well on the uneven bars and placing high in the beam, vault, and floor exercise. When the competition was over, only one other athlete finished with better individual scores. The sport had a new star.

In 1998, Jie continued to distinguish herself as the leader of China's newest group of young gymnasts, as the team won the World Cup. Among those following her lead were emerging stars Liu Xuan, Huang Mandan, Meng Fei, and Rao Meizhen. Jie herself wound up a terrific season by winning gold medals in the beam and bars at the China Cup, turning in a performance that the country's normally staid news agency called "spirited."

By international standards, Jie is still quite reserved. But as she is exposed to different people and places, experts believe she will add even more passion to her near-perfect technical skills. When that happens, look out! China's national coach, Qian Kui, confirms the belief of many in the sport that her prize pupil will soon become a force in gymnastics. She even predicts Jie will win gold medals in the beam and uneven bars in the Olympics. Quite simply, Qian says, Jie "is going to be a star."

Jie takes to the air during the 1998 Goodwill Games.

Svetlana Khorkina

E ver since the history-making performances of Olga Korbut and Nadia Comaneci, competitive gymnastics has been the exclusive realm of small, hard-bodied, pixie-like performers. In virtually every major country, supple, long-limbed athletes were either pushed into rhythmic gymnastics or steered away from the sport entirely. One girl—one tall, graceful, elegant girl—refused to listen. Her name is Svetlana Khorkina, and fans thank their lucky stars for her stubbornness every time she competes. "Against everyone's advice," she smiles, "I began doing the gymnastics that I liked."

Svetlana, or "Sveta," as she is called in Russia, was born in 1979. She became interested in a gymnastics career after watching the Soviet team mop up at the 1983 World Championships. Even at the tender age of four, it was clear that Svetlana did not have the classic gymnast's body. But she had something the other young hopefuls did not: spirit, stubbornness, and a wicked competitive streak.

Svetlana progressed quickly in the Russian gymnastics program, but as she grew taller than the other girls her age she had to fight against attempts to move her out of the all-around events and into rhythmic. Part of this battle was fought with the help of her coach, Boris Pilkin, who began working with her when she was seven. He tailored Svetlana's training and routines to complement her long limbs and slender physique. The idea was to make her height an advantage, not a disadvantage. To this day,

Svetlana twists during her gold-medal routine at the 1996 Olympics.

Bi Wenjiing (left) and Amy Chow flank Svetlana on the medal stand after the uneven bars competition at the 1996 Olympics.

Svetlana credits Pilkin with her success, and calls him her "second father." She knows he took a risk going against the system and sticking with her.

Nonsense, Pilkin responds. He knew all along she had what it took to be a champion. "As a child she was very interested in trying new things," he remembers. "She was very competitive. She understood her talent, and even her psychological strength. I told her that her future would be great."

Svetlana joined the Russian national team in 1992, at the age of 13. It was not until the following year, however, that she started to show her first flashes of brilliance. In 1993, Svetlana took five individual golds in the Baltic Sea Games and Russian Championships. Two of those came on the uneven bars, an event that she was quickly making her own. Every time she performed this event, a buzz went through the crowd while she jackknifed her 105 pound body and then stretched it to its full length of nearly 5' 4" as she performed her dramatic routine. Today, two moves she developed are named after her: Khorkina One and Khorkina Two.

At the 1994 European Championships, Svetlana finished second in the all-arounds and won a gold medal on the bars. She then claimed two more individual medals at the World Championships and three others at the Goodwill Games, including another gold-medal performance on the bars. She concluded her amazing year with a breathtaking interpretation of the opera *Carmen* during the floor exercise at the World Team Championships. It was a performance that brought fans close to tears.

Svetlana's next goal was to win a gold medal at the 1996 Olympics. This she did, with a stirring routine on the uneven bars. But Atlanta was a disappointment in other respects. The Unified Team, as athletes from Russia and other former Soviet Union states were now called, was upset by Team USA, and had to settle for the silver medal. And the all-around competition was a disaster for Svetlana, as she placed a shockingly low 15th.

Like a true champion, Svetlana came away from her Olympic experience with a positive attitude. Her poor finish in the all-arounds woke her

Getting Personal

Svetlana was born in Belgorod in the Soviet Union. The town is now part of Russia...Her sister's name is Yuliya, her mother's name is Lyubov, and her father's name is Vasili...Yuliya is also a gymnast—and a good one. She, too, may make the Russian national team...Svetlana tried rhythmic gymnastics for a year and hated it...Her parents separated several years ago, but she still speaks with her father often...Svetlana now lives in a training camp outside of Moscow, about 250 miles away from Belgorod...Never one to bow to convention, she shocked the gymnastics world in 1997 when she struck some provocative poses for a popular Russian men's magazine...Svetlana's best friend is fellow gymnast Yelena Grosheva. The two stars met as youngsters and rarely make a move without consulting...Svetlana is instantly recognized wherever she goes in Europe, which is why she was signed to endorse a well-known brand of wristwatches...She recently bought her first car, but has not had time to learn how to drive it.

Career *Highlights*

Year	Achievement
1993	Gold Medalist, Russian Championships, All-Arounds, Uneven Bars, & Balance Beam
1994	Gold Medalist, European Championships, Uneven Bars
1994	Gold Medalist, Goodwill Games, Uneven Bars & Team Competition
1995	Gold Medalist, Russian Championships, All-Around
1995	Gold Medalist, World Championships, Uneven Bars
1996	Gold Medalist, European Championships, Uneven Bars
1996	Gold Medalist, World Championships, Uneven Bars
1996	Olympic Gold Medalist, Uneven Bars
1996	Olympic Silver Medalist, Team Competition
1997	Gold Medalist, Russian Championships, All-Arounds & Uneven Bars
1997	Gold Medalist, World Championships, All-Arounds & Uneven Bars
1998	Gold Medalist, European Championships, All-Arounds

up to the fact that she was not consistent enough in two key areas: the floor exercise and the vault. She and her coach went to work to prepare for the 1997 World Championships.

When the competition rolled around, Svetlana was ready. She did well in the balance beam, held her own in the vault, and her floor exercise was superb. Going into the final event, she had the slimmest of leads over Simona Amanar. Luckily for Svetlana, the final event was her specialty, the uneven bars. Still, the pressure was on. Simona Amanar went before her and received excellent scores. Svetlana needed to be at her very best, or she would lose. The intensity of the moment seemed to energize her. She performed each move on the bars flawlessly and then nailed her dismount, prompting the loudest roar of the day from the audience. The gold medal was hers.

A half-dozen years of tough, international competition has made Svetlana a natural leader. In fact, she was recently named captain of the national team. Her advice to teammates? "One needs to be very artistic to express meaning and style," she tells them.

Her advice to fans trying to find her in the crowd? "I'm very easy to see on the podium," she chuckles, "because everyone else is *small*."

Such wit and wisdom typically comes from an athlete on the downside of her career. But Svetlana believes that, in her case, the best is yet to come. As she enters her twenties—"old age" for most women in her sport—she is most definitely on the upswing, with a lot more gold glittering in her future. "To tell you the truth," she says, "I do not think I have yet achieved my best."

Svetlana is so good on the bars that there are two moves named after her.

ON HER MIND

"I don't know how to describe how I am feeling...it is like a dream."

Kris Maloney

Little Kris Maloney hated to see her older siblings leave every morning. When Shawn and Carrie packed up and went to school, she felt left out and left behind. This became such a problem that her mother, Linda, decided to do something about it. "When I was young my mom placed me in classes so I'd have something to do," remembers Kris. "I was five years old."

Those classes were gymnastics classes, and she took to them in a big way. Before long, she was the best in her age group, and soon she was the best in the gym. When the family moved across the Delaware River from Hacketstown, New Jersey, to Pen Argyl, Pennsylvania, Kris was already getting serious about competing. After working with coaches Bill and Donna Strauss for a few years, she progressed to the point where she was ready to compete on a national basis.

Kris's first big season was 1993, when she was 12 years old. She placed a respectable 14th in the all-arounds in the junior division of the U.S. Championships, and finished second among juniors at the U.S. Classic. Kris even traveled overseas, competing in England at the Heathrow Gold Cup. The Strausses knew they had a special pupil on their hands when Kris rose to the occasion and finished first in the balance beam, vault, and all-arounds at this competition.

Kris shows the grace and style that made her U.S. champion on the balance beam in 1998.

When Kris added consistency to her athleticism, she became one of the best gymnasts in the world.

The next three years were spent refining Kris's skills and getting her used to competing against top gymnasts at both the junior and senior levels. In 1994—the year she first qualified for the national team— she finished first among juniors in the floor exercise at the U.S Classic and tied for second in this event at the U.S. Olympic Festival. In 1995, she competed in senior events, concentrating less on winning and more on learning. In 1996, Kris *used* what she learned to stand out at six major events, including the U.S. Championships, where she barely missed winning a medal in her specialty, the floor exercise. She was not quite Olympic caliber—she missed making the '96 team—but she was not far off.

Kris believed she was on the verge of becoming the country's top gymnast. Others in the sport were not so sure. They questioned if she had the toughness and commitment to become a champion. Unlike the other girls on the team, Kris had chosen to lead a more "normal" life. Although she trained as hard as the others, she did not give her life over to gymnastics, preferring to work her schedule around school, instead of vice versa. "I tried to listen to the good," says Kris, "and not all the people who thought I didn't have what it takes to win."

After the Olympics, six of the seven members of the U.S. team decided to take a break from elite competition. That left the door wide open to young guns like Kris, Vanessa Atler, Kristy Powell, Jamie Dantzscher, and Lindsay Wing. The 1997 season was an exciting one for all of these young women, as they pushed "veteran" Dominique Moceanu for supremacy on the team. When the smoke cleared, Kris seemed to have the slightest edge. At least, that is how USA Gymnastics saw it. The organization voted her its Sportswoman of the Year.

Kris could now do it all. She scored well in tough events like the vault and beam, improved her presentation in the floor exercise, and gained much-needed consistency in the uneven bars.

Getting Personal

Kris's full first name is Kristin, but when she was taught to write it in school, the teacher mistakenly told her to spell Kristen. She says either is okay...Her first idol was Nadia Comaneci. "I looked up to her a lot when I was little"...Kris is scheduled to graduate from high school in 1999. Her favorite subject is Spanish...Kris does not have much time to watch television, but she does have three favorite shows: DAWSON'S CREEK, PARTY OF FIVE and ALLY MCBEAL...She also has two cats, named Fluffy and Diddy, and a dog named Silkie...Kris has been a target for college recruiters since her sophomore year. Schools that expressed interest were Alabama, Florida, Georgia, and UCLA...Despite criticism about her commitment to gymnastics, going to a regular school has been important to Kris. "It's a way to keep my life balanced. Sometimes I get behind, but the teachers help me."

The 1998 season was Kris's coming out party. Shortly after her 17th birthday, she joined the U.S. team for the International Team Championships. This same group had lost to the powerful Romanians in 1997, confirming the fears of some fans that U.S. gymnastics might be on the decline. At this competition, however, Team USA was magnificent. "We rocked floor!" Kris recalls. "It was the best feeling I ever had."

Career *Highlights*

Year	Achievement
1994	Gold Medalist, U.S. Olympic Festival, Team Competition
1994	Silver Medalist, U.S. Olympic Festival, Floor Exercise
1997	Gymnast of the Year
1997	Sportswoman of the Year, USA Gymnastics
1997	Gold Medalist, American Classic, All-Arounds
1997	Silver Medalist, U.S. Championships, Vault
1997	Bronze Medalist, U.S. Championships, Floor Exercise
1997	Silver Medalist, International Team Championships
1998	Gymnast of the Year
1998	Sportswoman of the Year, USA Gymnastics
1998	Gold Medalist, Goodwill Games, Balance Beam
1998	Gold Medalist, American Classic, All-Arounds, Balance Beam, & Floor Exercise
1998	Gold Medalist, International Team Championships
1998	Gold Medalist, U.S. Championships, All-Arounds
1998	Gold Medalist, U.S. Championships, Balance Beam

At a pivotal point in the meet, with the Romanians and Chinese working on their best events, Kris had to come up big on the floor exercise. With the pressure on, she delivered one of the best performances of her life. "I went through my routine and it just felt like I was dreaming," she says. "And then it was done. I came down and I was mobbed by my teammates and coaches. It felt like it wasn't real."

It was real, all right. Not only had Kris clinched a huge win for Team USA, she also took first place in the all-arounds. From there, the season just got better. She placed first in the all-arounds at the American Classic and Pacific Alliance Championships, then won a gold medal on the balance beam at the Goodwill Games. Kris capped off her great year at the U.S. Championships, winning the all-around title and finishing in the top four in the beam, vault, bars, and floor exercise.

Anyone still wondering about the "toughness" of the U.S. team had their fears put to rest by Kris. She won her gold medals at the Nationals despite a stress fracture in her right leg. It was not considered serious enough to keep her out of competition, but every time she put pressure on the leg, flashes of pain shot through her body. "I was just worried about the landings," says Kris. "On my first vault I landed with the most pressure on my bad leg, which really hurt."

Fighting through an injury was a real education for Kris. She now knows that nothing short of a catastrophic physical setback can keep her from doing her best. It is just the confidence-booster she needs as the 2000 Olympics draw near. So is beating three former national all-around champions (Moceanu, Atler, and Kim Zmeskal) in head-to-head competition at the U.S. Championships—although that is not how Kris sees it.

"I didn't really think I was *beating* anyone," she says modestly. "I just wanted to hit all my routines."

Kris's international "coming out" party took place at the 1998 Goodwill Games, where she struck gold on the balance beam.

ON HER MIND

"You'll learn a lot of great lessons and how to set goals in gymnastics, but the main thing is you'll have fun."

Shannon Miller

T he greatest career in the history of American gymnastics began with a Christmas present. Four-year-old Shannon Miller and her older sister, Tessa, fell in love with the trampoline their parents gave them in December 1981. Unfortunately, the two rambunctious girls proceeded to scare the daylights out of Claudia and Ron Miller, who feared the kids would kill themselves. So they took away the trampoline and signed their daughters up for gymnastics classes. Shannon immediately distinguished herself as a girl who took instruction well and always wanted to move up to the next level.

In 1986, Shannon was part of a group of Oklahoma gymnasts visiting the Soviet Union. Her mother was approached by several Russian coaches, who told her that her daughter had tremendous potential, and that she should seek out the best training in her area when they returned to the United States.

On that same trip, Claudia Miller ran into Steve Nunno. He ran Dynamo Gymnastics in Oklahoma City, which was about 45 minutes from their home in Edmond, Oklahoma. Nunno had worked under Bela Karolyi, who coached Mary Lou Retton to a gold medal at the 1984 Olympics. Nunno recognized Shannon's potential and moved her into classes with older and more experienced girls. She responded beautifully, becoming one of the top juniors in the world by the age of 11.

Shannon finished second in the all-arounds at the Junior Pan Am Games in 1988 and won the uneven bars at the U.S. Olympic Festival in

*When you are a shade under five feet tall,
the giraffes have to come down to meet you!*

Shannon was on top of the world in 1996, when she won Olympic gold on the balance beam.

1989. In 1990, she distinguished herself in senior competition, winning the balance beam at the American Cup and the all-arounds, vault, beam, and floor exercise at the Catania Cup in Italy. She also made the national team that year. In 1991, 14-year-old Shannon helped Team USA finish second at the World Championships, and won an individual silver medal in the balance beam.

Working with Nunno and Team USA coach Peggy Liddick, Shannon began to focus on the 1992 Olympics. Though she had been the team's rising star in '91, in Barcelona she was not considered a major threat to win a medal. Teammate Kim Zmeskal had come into her own in 1992, and represented America's best hope of bringing home some hardware. Besides, Shannon had undergone elbow surgery that spring, and it was not clear whether she was back to full strength. "Other people may not have had high expectations for me in Barcelona, but I had high expectations for myself," she maintains.

And with good reason—while Zmeskal got a case of nerves and dropped out of sight, Shannon was in the zone! She won a silver medal in her specialty, the balance beam, a bronze in the uneven bars, and a bronze in the floor exercise. In the all-arounds, Shannon really put the heat on leader Tatiana Gutsu of the Unified Team. In fourth place going into the final event—the vault— Shannon tried a spinning, twisting Yurchenko layout and nailed it for a score of 9.975. Suddenly, she was in first place! It took the vault of Gutsu's career to regain the lead. Shannon would have liked a gold medal, but she was very pleased with the unexpected silver. Led by their new star, Team USA secured a bronze medal in the team competition, giving Shannon a total of five medals— a record for an American gymnast.

Shannon proved her Olympic showing was no fluke, winning 10 more gold medals in the U.S. and World Championships over the next

Getting Personal

As a baby, Shannon's legs were turned severely inward. She was fitted with corrective braces...Although she and Tessa began gymnastics together, her sister dropped out when the training intensified. She opted for art lessons instead...Shannon was lucky that her father could drive her to and from practice. A college professor, he arranged his classes around her schedule...Shannon attended a local high school throughout her career. To stay as normal as possible, she refused to talk about gymnastics in school...She credits Steve Nunno with getting the most out of her, and for teaching her how to "step back and take a look at the big picture," which she says has been the secret to achieving her goals...Shannon was a Sullivan Award nominee for best U.S. amateur athlete in 1993, '94 and '95...Being a celebrity has its disadvantages. Shannon believed she was being stalked at college in 1998, and after an investigation an arrest was eventually made.

four years. Instead of slowing down, as some gymnasts do when they reach their late teens, she kept getting better. Not surprisingly, Shannon began setting her sights on Atlanta. "I hadn't planned to keep competing until 1996," she admits, "but after the '92 Olympics were over, I didn't want to stop. It's so much fun!"

At the 1996 Olympics, Shannon led Team USA to a gold medal. She helped keep her teammates focused and set the stage for terrific performances in all of the events. "We couldn't have gotten the medal without

Career *Highlights*

Year	Achievement
1989	Gold Medalist, U.S. Olympic Festival, Uneven Bars
1990	Gold Medalist, American Classic, Balance Beam & Floor Exercise
1991	Gold Medalist, U.S. Championships, Balance Beam
1991	Silver Medalist, World Championships, Uneven Bars & Team Competition
1992	Gold Medalist, U.S. Olympic Trials, All-Arounds
1992	Olympic Bronze Medalist, Uneven Bars, Floor Exercise, & Team Competition
1992	Olympic Silver Medalist, All-Arounds & Balance Beam
1993	Gold Medalist, American Cup, All-Arounds, Vault, Uneven Bars, & Floor Exercise
1993	Gold Medalist, World Championships, All-Arounds, Uneven Bars, & Floor Exercise
1993	Gold Medalist, U.S. Olympic Festival, All-Arounds, Vault, Balance Beam, Floor Exercise, & Team Competition
1993	Gold Medalist, U.S. Championships, All-Arounds
1994	Gold Medalist, World Championships, All-Arounds, & Balance Beam
1994	Silver Medalist, Goodwill Games, All-Arounds, Vault, & Uneven Bars
1994	Gold Medalist, Goodwill Games, Balance Beam & Floor Exercise
1995	Gold Medalist, American Classic, All-Arounds
1995	Gold Medalist, U.S. Championships, Vault
1995	Gold Medalist, Pan Am Games, All-Arounds, Uneven Bars, Floor Exercise, & Team Competition
1995	Bronze Medalist, World Championships, Team Competition
1996	Gold Medalist, U.S. Championships, All-Arounds
1996	Olympic Gold Medalist, Balance Beam & Team Competition
1997	Gold Medalist, World University Games, All-Arounds
1997	Gold Medalist, International Gymnastics Cup, All-Arounds

any one person," says Shannon, downplaying her leadership role. "We all had to hit it the same day and at the same time."

After the "Magnificent Seven" accepted their gold medals, Shannon went out and gave a heart-stopping performance on the balance beam. For her extraordinary efforts, she was awarded the gold medal—her first individual gold in the Olympics, and the only individual gold won by the U.S. team in 1996. It was a fitting farewell.

Only it *wasn't* farewell. Shannon continued to compete, joining the team's gold medal tour of the United States and then entering several events in 1997. She finished first in the all-arounds at the Reese's

International Gymnastics Cup, and then won a gold medal in the all-arounds at the World University Games. In 1998, Shannon concentrated on her studies at the University of Oklahoma, and on her personal life. She and boyfriend Chris Phillips announced their engagement in September.

It seems impossible, but we may see Shannon in the Olympics again. Her fans insist that she could make the 2000 team, although she says there is no chance. But Shannon has taken up another sport—*figure skating*—and she is already pretty good. Who knows, if she doesn't pull on a leotard in Sydney, she might lace up the skates in Salt Lake City!

Shannon was the only member of the U.S. team to capture a gold medal in an individual event at the 1996 Olympics.

ON HER MIND

"I like how kids enjoy watching me perform. They're enthusiastic and that makes it fun."

Dominique
Moceanu

Can someone be a "born" gymnast? Dominique Moceanu comes pretty close. Before emigrating to the United States the year before Dominique was born, Dumitru and Camelia Moceanu were gymnasts in their native Romania. They decided that if their first child showed any aptitude for the sport, they would do whatever they could to make her a champion. Most parents would have waited until their daughter turned two or three before "testing" her, but the Moceanus just could not wait. When Dominique was six months old, they strung a clothesline across their kitchen, then picked her up and let her grab it. Camelia waited beneath Dominique to catch her when she fell, but she never let go. "My parents say they knew then that I had what it took," she smiles.

When Dominique turned three, her father contacted fellow Romanian Bela Karolyi, who had a training center in Houston, Texas. Karolyi laughed when Dumitru asked him to take his daughter, and suggested he call back when she was nine. "Let the kid grow up," he told Dumitru.

The family moved from their home in California to the suburbs of Chicago. It was there, in Highland Park, that Dominique first began taking gymnastics lessons. A year later, in 1985, the Moceanus moved again, to Tampa, Florida. Dominique enrolled at LaFleur's Gymnastics, and started making great strides. At the age of seven, she entered her first

Dominique stretches before a workout.

Dominique and Bela Karolyi formed one of the most remarkable teams in the history of the sport.

competition. Although she did not win, she remembers hearing the applause and liking it. She resolved to do better from that point on.

Dominique improved so dramatically—and so quickly—that she soon outgrew LaFleur's. Her father contacted Karolyi and reminded him of their conversation several years earlier. The coach agreed to take Dominique on as a pupil.

This was more of a gamble for the Moceanu family than for Karolyi. Her parents had jobs in Tampa; Dominique and her younger sister, Christina, were already in school. They would all be starting again from scratch. "I couldn't believe it when I heard my dad say that we were moving to Houston," Dominique recalls. "It seemed unreal."

Karolyi's gym was like a dream come true for 10-year-old Dominique. She now had access to the best coaching staff in country, and her classmates included Kerri Strug, Kim Zmeskal, and Betty Okino—all world-class gymnasts. Dominique was told that she would have to forget everything she had learned and start over, for only with sound fundamentals could she develop into an international competitor. Some believed that it would take years for her to get to that level, but in just seven months she qualified for the junior division of the U.S. Championships. No 10-year-old had ever done that before. Dominique not only qualified, she won a gold medal in the balance beam!

Getting Personal

At the 1993 Juniors, Dominique finished seventh in the all-arounds. By 1994, Karolyi had removed the rough edges from her technique and molded his young prodigy into an amazingly mature competitor. He also infused Dominique with the confidence she needed. "Bela told me that if I really worked hard and pushed myself, I could achieve my biggest dreams," she says.

With the Olympics just two years away, the '94 U.S. Championships were considered a key competition for American gymnastics. In the senior division, Team USA's leaders would emerge; in the junior division, the hope was that a promising youngster might distinguish herself and "fast-track" to the Olympic squad.

No one, however, could have expected what happened next. Dominique wiped out her fellow juniors, winning the all-around competition and taking gold in the floor exercise and the vault. She won with the style and swagger of an athlete half again as old. Everyone in Nashville that day agreed: there had to be a much older person "hiding" in that 12-year-old body.

In 1995, Dominique moved up to senior competition and won a silver medal on the beam at the World Championships. It was the only individual medal won by an American at the event. Dominique also finished first in the all-arounds at the World Team Trials and Visa Challenge—both elite-level meets. At the U.S. Championships, she established herself as America's top gymnast, finishing first in the all-arounds, second in the

Career *Highlights*

Year	Achievement
1991	Gold Medalist, U.S. Junior Championships, Balance Beam
1992	Gold Medalist, Junior Pan Am Games, Team Competition
1994	Gold Medalist, U.S. Junior Championships, All-Arounds, Vault, & Floor Exercise
1995	Gold Medalist, U.S. Championships, All-Arounds
1996	Olympic Gold Medalist, Team Competition
1998	Gold Medalist, U.S. Championships, Vault, & Balance Beam
1998	Gold Medalist, Goodwill Games, All-Arounds

floor exercise and third in the vault. "It was incredible to be the national champion," she says. "All my hard work in the gym paid off."

Unfortunately, what should have been a stellar 1996 season began with pain and uncertainty. Prior to to the Olympic trials, Dominique began experiencing severe pain in her right leg. That summer, X-rays revealed a stress fracture to her tibia, which meant she had to stop training. With Dominique in jeopardy of missing the Olympics, Karolyi petitioned the Olympic Committee to put her on the seven-woman team based on her great scores at the '95 nationals. The governing body agreed, provided that no more than six competitors at the trials scored higher. Dominique had to sweat out four rotations before she knew for sure that she had made it.

By the Olympics, the pain in Dominique's leg had subsided enough to compete. She unveiled a brand, new floor routine before the crowd in Atlanta. Set to the song *The Devil Went Down to Georgia*, it brought the house down. Team USA was on a roll at this point, and was building up a formidable lead. Going into the final team event, the vault, everyone just needed to land their jumps to ensure the gold medal. Everything was going well, with Dominique and Kerri Strug the only two left. The Russians were on the floor exercise, an event where they figured to score well. Incredibly, Dominique fell on both of her vaults. Despite her mistakes, Team USA seemed to have mathematically assured itself of the gold medal. But no one could be absolutely sure. Dominique felt terrible as she watched Strug hurt herself on her first attempt, then make her second vault with a badly injured ankle. "That meant a lot to all of us," Dominique says.

After the Olympics, Bela Karolyi retired. "It was really nice having him around," says Dominique. "He was a lot of fun and he taught me a lot."

In 1997 and 1998, Dominique's biggest challenge was contending with her changing body. She was getting taller and heavier—which meant she had to continually adjust her routines—and the stress of training led to a series of painful injuries. Still, she stayed at the top of her sport, placing second in the floor exercise at the 1997 nationals, winning gold in the all-arounds at the 1998 Goodwill Games, and scoring first-place finishes in the vault and balance beam at the '98 U.S. Championships.

Though she is now considered a competition-hardened veteran, Dominique has lost none of the luster she brought to the world of gymnastics in the mid-1990s. Her sense of humor and playful personality still come through in her routines, as does her supreme confidence. Hopefully, her delightful smile will continue to light up the sport well into the 21st century.

Dominique grew several inches after the 1996 Olympics. She has had to "re-learn" many of the routines she was once able to so easily master.

What's Next

P rior to the 1996 Olympics, elite-level gymnasts could expect to win a few trophies and medals, earn a college scholarship, and perhaps snare a commercial endorsement or two. The revenue they generated as performers, however, rarely found its way into their pockets. After the Olympics, this began to change. The marketing machine that had geared up to promote the '96 games kept chugging along, transforming the gold medalists into high-demand superstars. There were tours and books and commercials and public appearances and, suddenly, millions of dollars.

With all that money, however, there came a heavy price. In the years since the "Magnificent Seven's" gold-medal performance, the sport's image has lost some of its luster. What the world now sees when it looks upon the face of gymnastics are scars and blemishes. They were always there—it was simply the money that brought this ugliness to the surface.

Dominique Moceanu's legal action against her mother and father (see page 59) was a shock to her fans. She appeared to be living the life every athlete in her sport dreams about. Then the public began hearing whispers about other gymnasts who had sought legal remedies to problems with their parents. Was this a disturbing trend, or just a few isolated incidents? The fact is, back when young women competed solely for personal pride and national honor, bungling, over-bearing parents were simply nuisances. Now they are viewed as financial liabilities. Dominique was not the first to resort to an extreme solution, and she will not be the last.

Meanwhile, other controversies within the sport have come to light. The trend toward pushing young girls too hard too soon may be remedied somewhat by the minimum age requirements of international competition, but that may not be the case for long. Sooner or later, a super-talented 15-year-old with a high-powered legal team will sue the sport to allow her to compete. If she wins (and she probably will), then the insanity will begin all over again, and coaches will be pushing 9-, 10- and 11-year-olds even harder.

The minimum age requirement has also created a problem potentially as complex as the one it was designed to solve. Judges, it seems, still reserve their highest marks for the kind of risky, acrobatic maneuvers that are much easier for 13- and 14-year-olds to perform. At the elite level, this situation is already causing considerable anxiety. Dominique Moceanu is a perfect case in point. She is now six inches taller and several pounds heavier than she was at 14, and would have a tough time duplicating some of the moves she used to win the U.S. all-around title in 1995. As she prepares for the 2000 Olympics and beyond, should she be re-learning those old moves, or concentrating on perfecting the ones that now come more naturally? Hopefully, this question will be answered soon. Gymnastics is a contact sport, and the older an athlete gets, the more at risk she is of suffering a career-ending injury.

For the many thousands of girls who would die to swap places with Dominique, the issues are more profound. Indeed, a handful of young gymnasts *have* died pursuing this dream. Bulimia and anorexia run rampant at all levels of the sport (studies suggest more than half of the world's top gymnasts suffer from an eating disorder), and accidents in training and at meets have permanently crippled—and even killed—competitors.

Fortunately, there appears to be a genuine concern over safety in gymnastics, which bodes well for the sport. An acceptable balance will no doubt be struck between risk and reward, and gymnastics will continue to flourish. Perhaps two divisions will be created, one for women and one for girls. What direction the sport takes in the 21st century—and what kind of marvelous new athletes it produces—should make for one of the most compelling stories in all of women's sports.

INDEX

PAGE NUMBERS IN ITALICS REFER TO ILLUSTRATIONS.